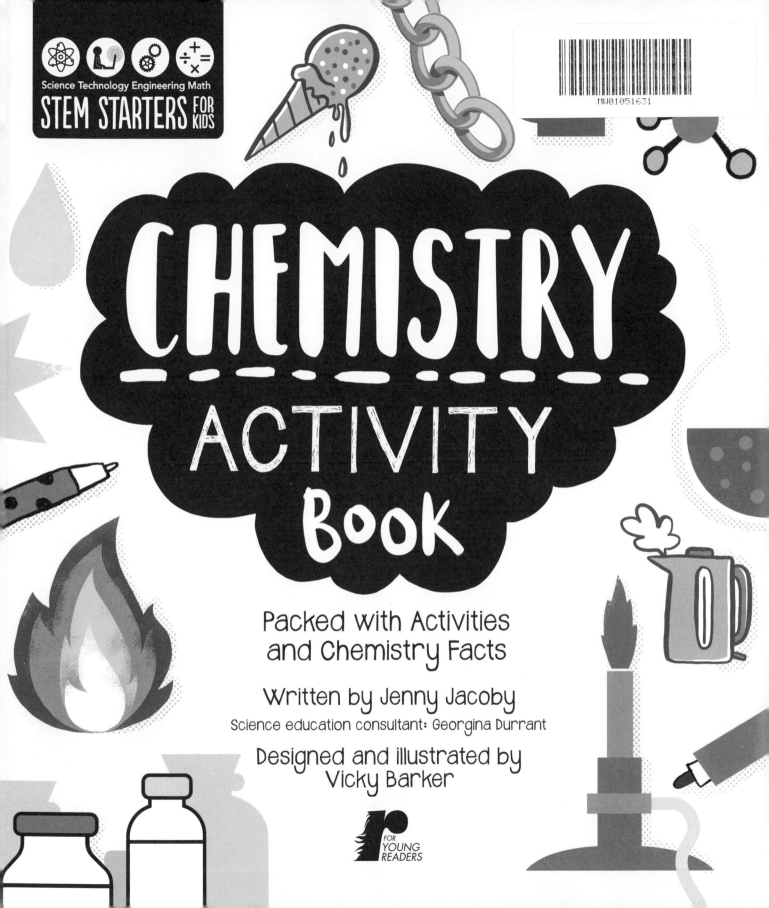

Science Technology Engineering Math
STEM STARTERS FOR KIDS

CHEMISTRY
ACTIVITY
Book

Packed with Activities
and Chemistry Facts

Written by Jenny Jacoby

Science education consultant: Georgina Durrant

Designed and illustrated by
Vicky Barker

FOR
YOUNG
READERS

Racehorse for Young Readers books may be purchased in bulk at special discounts for sales promotions, corporate gifts, fund-raising or education purposes. Special editions can also be created to specifications. For details, contact the Special Sales Department at Skyhorse Publishing, 307 West 36th Street, 11th Floor, New York, NY 10018 or info@skyhorsepublishing.com.

Racehorse for Young Readers is a pending trademark of Skyhorse Publishing, Inc.®, a Delaware corporation.

Visit our website at skyhorsepublishing.com

10 9 8 7 6 5 4 3 2 1

Design and art direction by Vicky Barker
Science education consultant: Georgina Durrant

Printed in China

Text and illustrations copyright © b small publishing 2020

First Racehorse for Young Readers Edition 2020

ISBN
978-1-63158-641-5

WHAT IS CHEMISTRY?

Chemistry is the part of science to do with materials and substances, what they are made out of, how they behave and how they work together. Sometimes chemistry involves putting substances together in a test tube and making things go BANG, but chemicals are all around us, not just in a laboratory.

WHAT IS STEM?

STEM stands for "science, technology, engineering and mathematics." These four areas are closely linked, and chemistry is an important part of the science area. If we understand what the materials around us are made from and how they react, we will know how they can be useful and safe. Technology and engineering, with chemistry, can help us make the most of the materials in the world.

Science

Technology

Engineering

Math

WHAT IS A CHEMICAL?

Chemicals don't just live in sealed bottles in chemistry labs. Chemicals are all around us! Chemicals can be found in nature (such as salt) or man-made (such as plastic). Even our bodies are made up of chemicals! Not just our blood, spit, and all the juicy parts inside, but all the hard parts too, like our bones, organs, and hair.

Some chemicals are dangerous but most are very safe. One way the power of a chemical can be measured is the pH scale. It measures whether a chemical is acidic or alkaline. Chemicals at either end of the scale are very strong and dangerous to handle. Chemicals in the middle of the scale are neutral and are safe.

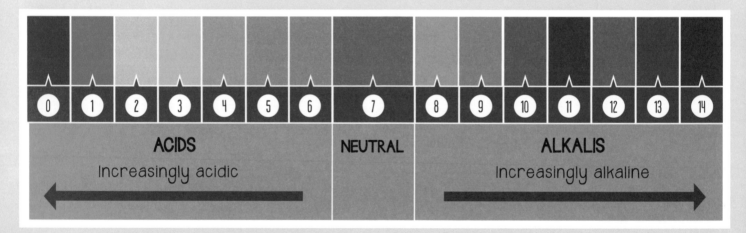

| 0 | 1 | 2 | 3 | 4 | 5 | 6 | 7 | 8 | 9 | 10 | 11 | 12 | 13 | 14 |

ACIDS
Increasingly acidic

NEUTRAL

ALKALIS
Increasingly alkaline

DID YOU KNOW?

Your stomach is full of powerful acid! It's there to help with digestion. Your stomach is specially made to cope with the acid, but if the acid comes into your throat you can feel a burning sensation.

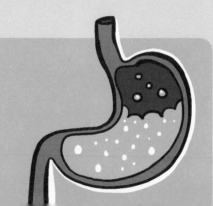

Use the pH scale color guide to write the correct pH on each of these bottles of chemicals. Then choose the correct label from below for each shelf. Answers on page 30.

LABELS

Weak alkalis

Weak acids

Neutral

WARNING:
Strong alkalis

WARNING:
Strong acids

1

A SULPHURIC ACID

pH

STOMACH ACID

pH

2

BLEACH

pH

AMMONIA

pH

3

PURE WATER

pH

BLOOD

pH

4

VINEGAR

pH

ORANGE JUICE

pH

5

BAKING SODA

pH

EGGS

pH

CHEMICAL SAFETY

In the chemistry lab, safety is vital. How can you tell what is a dangerous acid and what is simply water? Not by drinking it! One way to understand different chemicals is to observe them using your senses. But safety is always the most important thing.

DOs

- ALWAYS READ AND FOLLOW THE INSTRUCTIONS

- WEAR GLOVES AND GOGGLES AND A LAB COAT

- USE YOUR EYES TO OBSERVE COLOR AND TRANSPARENCY

- USE YOUR HAND TO WAFT SAFE GASES AWAY FROM A CHEMICAL TOWARDS YOU TO OBSERVE THE SMELL

- LISTEN FOR ANY SOUNDS COMING FROM THE CHEMICALS

- WIPE UP ANY SPILLS IMMEDIATELY

DON'Ts

- NEVER TEST A CHEMICAL BY TASTE

- NEVER EAT IN THE LABORATORY

- NEVER LEAN YOUR FACE RIGHT OVER A CHEMICAL

- NEVER TOUCH ANY CHEMICALS DIRECTLY

- DO NOT RUN IN THE LABORATORY

Some of these ways of observing are good techniques and some should never be done in a chemistry lab. Circle the best practices and cross out those you should never do.
Answers on page 30.

MEASURING

There are lots of tools in a chemistry lab to help find out a bit more about the characteristics of different chemicals.

100 ML

Measuring cylinders

come in different sizes and can accurately measure small amounts of liquid.

A glass thermometer

can sit in a beaker of liquid to measure its temperature while it's being heated or cooled.

°C

Litmus paper

measures the acidity of a liquid. The paper turns a color that can be matched with the pH scale chart.

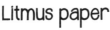

A balance

acts like accurate weighing-scales to measure the mass (how much it weighs) of a substance.

12 g

Read the measurements of each of these pieces of equipment and write your answers in.

Check your results on page 30.

Liquid in measuring cylinder : _____ ml

pH level on litmus paper : pH _____

Temperature of liquid in jar : _____ °C

Weight on scale : _____ g

9

WHAT'S THE MATTER?

"Matter" is the scientific word for "what things are made of." At the moment, we know of 118 different **elements** on Earth. That's just 118 different substances that combine in different ways to make up all known matter.

At the very smallest level, these elements are made up of **atoms.** Atoms are so small you can't see them even with a microscope. Only special electron microscopes can do that.

Atoms are rarely found on their own. Usually they combine with others to make **molecules.** A molecule can be as simple as two oxygen atoms bonded together, or a very complicated combination of hundreds or thousands of atoms, some with very strong double bonds between them.

Did you know?

The word "atom" comes from the Greek meaning "cannot be divided" to reflect that you can't divide an atom into anything smaller. However, at the end of the nineteenth century scientists realized that atoms were made up of even smaller particles, called **protons** (positive charges), **neutrons** (neutral charges) and **electrons** (negative charges). Today scientists are still investigating the nature of even smaller parts of atoms.

We know of more than 70 million different chemical compounds!

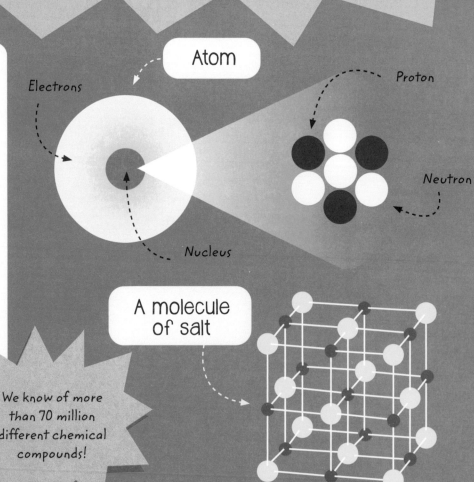

Atom

Electrons

Proton

Neutron

Nucleus

A molecule of salt

Use the color keys of each atom to give the right colors to each molecule.

Answers on page 30.

 Hydrogen Oxygen Carbon

Carbon dioxide
(the gas we breathe out)

O — C — O

Graphite
(pencil 'lead')

```
      C
   C     C

   C     C
      C
```

Oxygen
(the gas we breathe in)

O — O

Methane
(the smelly bit of a fart)

```
    H
    |
H — C — H
    |
    H
```

Water

```
   O
  / \
 H   H
```

Glucose
(sugar)

```
        H           H  H  H
        |           |  |  |
    O   O   H   O   O   O
     \  |   |   |   |   |
  O   C — C — C — C — C — C — H
  |   |       |   |   |   |
  H   H       O   H   H   H
              |
              H
```

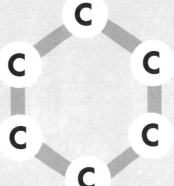

THE PERIODIC TABLE

Scientists organize the 118 elements into a table called the **Periodic Table.** Each element has its own square in the table, and the elements are ordered from the smallest to the largest.

The table is also arranged so that elements in each column have similar characteristics. By looking at where an element sits in the periodic table, a scientist can have an idea about how that element behaves.

group → period ↓	1	2	3
1	1 H		
2	3 Li	4 Be	
3	11 Na	12 Mg	
4	19 K	20 Ca	21 Sc
5	37 Rb	38 Sr	39 Y
6	55 Cs	56 Ba	57 La
7	87 Fr	88 Ra	89 Ac

Work out the sum to find the atomic number for each chemical. Write the chemical symbol from the periodic table opposite in the white circle. Look up their full names on page 32.

2.

$10 - 8 =$ ____

The gas that is used to make balloons float.

4.

$20 \div 2 =$ ____

A gas that can glow in fluorescent colors and is used in lights you might see in a city at night.

1.

$15 - 4 =$ ____

An element that is highly reactive, but when it combines the element at

$15 + 2 =$ ____

it makes the very common substance salt.

3.

$3 \times 2 =$ ____

One of the most common elements in the world, which is part of every one of your cells, as well as the pencils you draw with.

5.

$4 + 4 =$ ____

The element that your body needs from every breath you take.

12

What gives an atom its size? That's down to the number of protons in the nucleus (the central part). The number of protons is the 'atomic number'. Helium has one proton and its atomic number is one. All helium atoms have one proton.

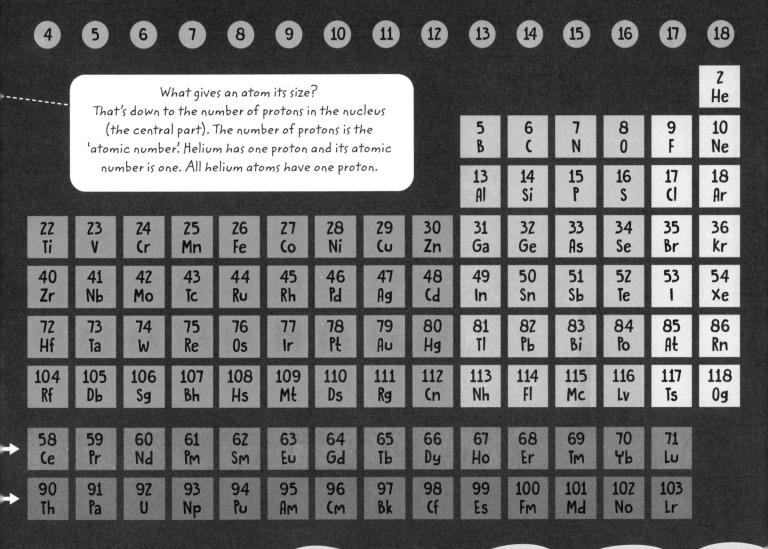

																	2 He
											5 B	6 C	7 N	8 O	9 F	10 Ne
											13 Al	14 Si	15 P	16 S	17 Cl	18 Ar
22 Ti	23 V	24 Cr	25 Mn	26 Fe	27 Co	28 Ni	29 Cu	30 Zn	31 Ga	32 Ge	33 As	34 Se	35 Br	36 Kr
40 Zr	41 Nb	42 Mo	43 Tc	44 Ru	45 Rh	46 Pd	47 Ag	48 Cd	49 In	50 Sn	51 Sb	52 Te	53 I	54 Xe
72 Hf	73 Ta	74 W	75 Re	76 Os	77 Ir	78 Pt	79 Au	80 Hg	81 Tl	82 Pb	83 Bi	84 Po	85 At	86 Rn
104 Rf	105 Db	106 Sg	107 Bh	108 Hs	109 Mt	110 Ds	111 Rg	112 Cn	113 Nh	114 Fl	115 Mc	116 Lv	117 Ts	118 Og

58 Ce	59 Pr	60 Nd	61 Pm	62 Sm	63 Eu	64 Gd	65 Tb	66 Dy	67 Ho	68 Er	69 Tm	70 Yb	71 Lu
90 Th	91 Pa	92 U	93 Np	94 Pu	95 Am	96 Cm	97 Bk	98 Cf	99 Es	100 Fm	101 Md	102 No	103 Lr

6.

$21 - 8 =$ _____

The element that makes up kitchen foil.

7.

$40 \div 2 =$ _____

An element found in your teeth and bones.

8.

$27 \div 3 =$ _____

The element to help keep your teeth strong (you might find it in your toothpaste).

Answers on page 30.

STATES OF MATTER

Matter is usually in one of three states: solid, liquid or gas.

Solids hold their shape.

Liquids can be poured and they either fit the shape of their container or form a pool.

Gases fill their container or escape from an unsealed container.

The reason solids, liquids and gases behave as they do is because of what their molecules (combination of atoms) are doing.

In a solid, the molecules are all in a fixed position next to their neighbors, but each molecule vibrates in its place.

In a liquid, the molecules move freely around each other.

In a gas, the molecules actively move about freely in the air.

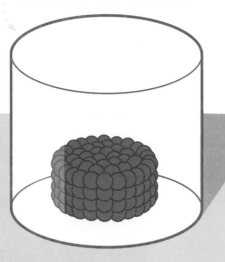

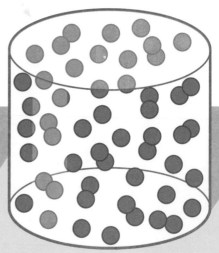

Did you know that some solids act like very thick liquids?
In very old houses, the panes of glass are sometimes thicker at the bottom, because over a very long time the glass has slowly been moving downwards due to gravity.

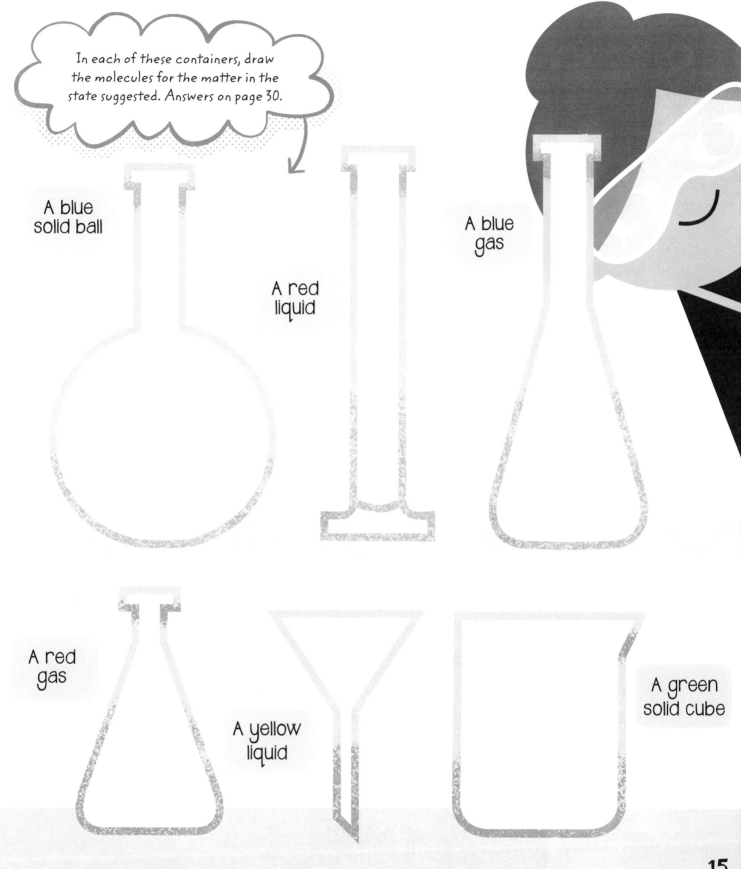

In each of these containers, draw the molecules for the matter in the state suggested. Answers on page 30.

A blue solid ball

A red liquid

A blue gas

A red gas

A yellow liquid

A green solid cube

SOLID SHAPES

We know that liquids and gases change their shape to fit their container. Solids hold their fixed shape so if we want to change their shape we need to use tools to mould them. But not all solids behave in the same way.

In **crystalline** solids, the bonds between the molecules are strong and even, so when they melt, the bonds melt evenly, and when they're cut, the surfaces are smooth and the edges straight.

wax candle

rock salt

In **amorphous** solids, the bonds between molecules are not even. Some break or melt before others. This means amorphous solids make less strong materials, and they can be moulded into different shapes.

Metals are, for the most part, crystalline solids but they can be pulled into different shapes.

Crystalline solids can be used in different ways from amorphous solids. Can you identify which is which by seeing how people are changing their shape?
Write either A or C in the circles. Answers on page 31.

MAKING MORE

Chemicals can be a solid, a liquid or a gas, but they aren't fixed in that state. Chemicals react to the temperature around them. If it gets warmer, the molecules get more energy, and if it gets colder, they have less energy. More energy means the molecules move more and if they move enough they can change from a solid into a liquid, or from a liquid into a gas.

When chemicals become colder, the molecules lose energy and move less quickly, and this change of speed can change a gas into a liquid or a liquid into a solid.

Gas becoming liquid is called **condensation**

Liquid becoming solid is called **solidification (or freezing)**

Solid becoming liquid is called **melting**

Liquid becoming gas is called **evaporation**

What happens to sugar that dissolves into a hot cup of tea? Does it disappear? No! You might not be able to see the sugar any more but your tongue can taste that the sugar is still in the liquid. The solid has melted into the liquid and the sugar molecules are now flowing freely around the other molecules that make up the cup of tea.

Changes of state happen all around us, every day. Draw or write what happens to these items when the temperature changes. Answers on page 31.

1.

2.

3.

4.

CHEMICAL CHANGES

Unlike melting and freezing, some chemical changes are irreversible: once they've happened, the chemical has been altered for ever.

Think about two activities that might happen in your kitchen:

To make a cup of tea → water is heated and turned into steam.

To cook an egg → an egg is cracked into a hot pan. → It changes color and texture.

The steam can return to liquid water when it cools down, but the egg cannot be uncooked.
This is called an **irreversible change**.

Burning causes irreversible changes. Matches can only be used once! Logs in a fire can only be burned once and houses that have burned down cannot be rebuilt reusing the same materials.

This is because the "fuel" that burns is chemically altered by being on fire. Wood starts off as a mixture of chemicals made up from carbon, oxygen, hydrogen and other elements. When it burns, the carbon, oxygen and hydrogen are released in smoke, and the solids left behind are char (almost pure carbon), and ash (everything unburnable that was in the wood).

This wood cannot be put back together again!

WATER

Quite simply the most important chemical on Earth, no life would be possible without water. Water is a vital ingredient in chemistry too. Here are some amazing water facts.

Water is made of two elements: hydrogen and oxygen.

Water is tasteless, transparent and odorless.

Water is the second most common molecule in the universe (after hydrogen).

Hot water freezes faster than cold water but nobody knows why!

Pure water is pH 7, which is neutral, meaning it's neither acidic nor alkaline.

Earth looks blue from space because water covers 71% of its surface.

Water is colored very slightly blue.

Sound travels more than four times faster in water than in air.

Water expands when it freezes and becomes less dense, which is why ice floats in water.

The human brain is made of 70% water.

A person can live for a month without food but only three days without water.

Water can dissolve more substances than any other liquid.

22

Water is everywhere!
In this scene, can you find:

- 7 glasses of water
- A river
- A waterfall
- 5 ducks
- Someone drinking from a water bottle
- 2 birds having a bath
- A pot of tea
- Ice cubes
- A dog drinking
- Spaghetti cooking
- Dishes being washed
- Children cooling down

Answers on page 31.

BIOCHEMISTRY

Biochemistry is the chemistry of living things.
There is a lot of chemistry that helps us to live.

Breathing

We breathe to bring oxygen into our lungs and let carbon dioxide out. Everything our body does requires oxygen and produces carbon dioxide as a waste product.

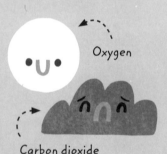

Oxygen

Carbon dioxide

Chewing

A chemical called amylase in your saliva (spit) helps break down food as you chew into chemicals your body can use more easily.

Amylase

Digesting

Acid in your stomach and bile in your intestines are just two of the many different chemicals that break food down into smaller and smaller pieces that your body can absorb and use.

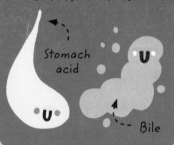

Stomach acid

Bile

Moving

Blood moves around your body carrying oxygen and glucose (the chemical that gives energy) so your muscles can move.

Glucose

Thinking

Even your brain needs chemicals to do all its thinking. Chemical messengers move from one nerve cell to another to pass on a message. The way the millions of brain nerve cells communicate is how you think the infinite different things you can think.

Neurotransmitters

Emotions

When you see something you like — perhaps a cute dog walking down the street — a special chemical messenger called dopamine is released in the brain, which gives you a sense of happiness.

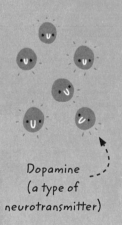

Dopamine (a type of neurotransmitter)

Help to put these cartoon chemicals in the right place in the body. Draw lines from the chemical to their home. Some of them might have more than one home! Answers on page 31.

METALS

Metals are a special group of elements. There are 91 metals on the periodic table and although they have different characteristics, there are some things all metals have in common:

- **Luster** – meaning they all shine in a particular "metallic" way
- **Flexibility** – they can be moulded and shaped even when solid
- **Conductivity** – electricity and heat can travel through them
- **Ductility** – they can be pulled into wire-shapes with the right machinery

Copper is made into pipes because it is strong and flexible and made into wires because it conducts electricity so well.

Zinc coats objects made from iron and steel to stop them rusting.

Nuts and bolts are made from iron because it is so strong.

Airplanes are made from aluminium because it is strong but also light.

Can you find these chemistry words in this word search?
Words can read backwards, forwards, up, down and diagonally.

```
s  t  h  j  d  e  l  o  s  p  h  d  e  p  h  v  l
y  i  m  a  g  n  e  s  i  u  m  c  g  y  u  v  p
k  t  l  y  t  a  r  k  u  d  e  a  i  r  f  n  l
c  g  m  v  c  r  u  i  n  t  o  l  t  u  a  c  a
a  u  e  o  e  m  i  t  o  d  a  u  e  c  r  t  y
b  n  z  i  n  r  e  o  u  d  t  m  s  r  t  j  t
t  l  s  y  l  e  a  d  t  s  i  i  h  e  f  s  l
i  a  w  g  i  e  u  o  c  o  d  n  l  m  v  a  i
n  t  v  n  a  g  o  e  r  d  d  i  e  a  o  e  t
f  e  o  r  h  p  a  e  s  i  n  u  b  g  l  i  h
h  r  t  u  k  j  v  l  o  u  a  m  u  n  c  e  i
i  e  p  l  y  g  r  p  a  m  p  n  g  h  r  t  u
c  k  c  o  p  p  e  r  s  t  z  i  n  c  n  l  m
d  s  o  i  s  d  f  d  s  z  e  z  a  i  o  u  r
j  y  g  l  j  t  s  o  s  a  m  g  o  l  d  y  c
l  p  l  a  t  i  n  u  m  e  x  e  c  s  i  k  j
f  e  o  c  u  p  y  s  e  o  d  a  v  i  r  o  a
```

ALUMINIUM   **LEAD**   **MERCURY**   **IRON**

COPPER   **LITHIUM**   **PLATINUM**   **SODIUM**

GOLD   **MAGNESIUM**   **SILVER**

TIN   **ZINC**

Answers on page 31.

27

CHEMICAL TESTS

Knowing a few facts about how different chemicals behave can be the key to unlocking a chemistry mystery.

Oxygen

Fire needs oxygen to burn. If something is burning, oxygen is around. If there is a lot of oxygen, the flames can burn well but if there is no oxygen the flame will go out.

Copper

burns with a green flame.

Potassium

burns with a lilac colored flame.

Carbon dioxide

is one of many gases that can be used to put out flames and fires.

Lithium

burns with a crimson red flame.

Hydrogen

If set on fire, hydrogen gas ignites with a squeaky pop sound.

Magnesium

burns with a bright white flame.

Use your chemistry knowledge to answer these questions.

1. Which candle will burn for longest?
2. Label each of these flames with the metal it is burning.
Answers on page 31.

1.

a

b

c

d

2.

29

ANSWERS

pages 4-5

1. STRONG ACIDS
2. STRONG ALKALIS
3. NEUTRAL
4. WEAK ACIDS
5. WEAK ALKALIS

A sulphuric acid	pH 1	Stomach acid	pH 2
Bleach	pH 13	Ammonia	pH 12
Pure water	pH 7	Blood	pH 7
Vinegar	pH 3	Orange juice	pH 4
Baking soda	pH 9	Eggs	pH 8

pages 10-11

pages 6-7

pages 12-13

1. **11 = Na** - Sodium
   17 = Cl - Chlorine
2. **2 = He** - Helium
3. **6 = C** - Carbon
4. **10 = Ne** - Neon
5. **8 = O** - Oxygen
6. **13 = Al** - Aluminium
7. **20 = Ca** - Calcium
8. **9 = F** - Fluorine

pages 14- 15

A solid blue ball

A red liquid

A blue gas

A red gas

A yellow liquid

A solid green cube

pages 8-9

Liquid in measuring cylinder : **70 ml**
pH level on litmus paper : **pH 3**
Temperature of liquid in jar : **55°C**
Weight on scale : **12 g**

pages 16-17

C

A

pages 18-19

1. Baked cake.
2. Clear path - hot water melts the ice.
3. Dry pavement - sun dries up the puddle.
4. Melted ice cream!

pages 20-21

pages 22-23

pages 24-25

pages 26-27

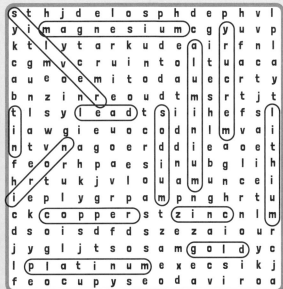

pages 28-29

1. C
2. From left to right

LITHIUM
MAGNESIUM
POTASSIUM
COPPER

31

1	**H** - Hydrogen	31	**Ga** - Gallium	61	**Pm** - Promethium	91	**Pa** - Protactinium
2	**He** - Helium	32	**Ge** - Germanium	62	**Sm** - Samarium	92	**U** - Uranium
3	**Li** - Lithium	33	**As** - Arsenic	63	**Eu** - Europium	93	**Np** - Neptunium
4	**Be** - Beryllium	34	**Se** - Selenium	64	**Gd** - Gadolinium	94	**Pu** - Plutonium
5	**B** - Boron	35	**Br** - Bromine	65	**Tb** - Terbium	95	**Am** - Americium
6	**C** - Carbon	36	**Kr** - Krypton	66	**Dy** - Dysprosium	96	**Cm** - Curium
7	**N** - Nitrogen	37	**Rb** - Rubidium	67	**Ho** - Holmium	97	**Bk** - Berkelium
8	**O** - Oxygen	38	**Sr** - Strontium	68	**Er** - Erbium	98	**Cf** - Californium
9	**F** - Fluorine	39	**Y** - Yttrium	69	**Tm** - Thulium	99	**Es** - Einsteinium
10	**Ne** - Neon	40	**Zr** - Zirconium	70	**Yb** - Ytterbium	100	**Fm** - Fermium
11	**Na** - Sodium	41	**Nb** - Niobium	71	**Lu** - Lutetium	101	**Md** - Mendelevium
12	**Mg** - Magnesium	42	**Mo** - Molybdenum	72	**Hf** - Hafnium	102	**No** - Nobelium
13	**Al** - Aluminium	43	**Tc** - Technetium	73	**Ta** - Tantalum	103	**Lr** - Lawrencium
14	**Si** - Silicon	44	**Ru** - Ruthenium	74	**W** - Tungsten	104	**Rf** - Rutherfordium
15	**P** - Phosphorus	45	**Rh** - Rhodium	75	**Re** - Rhenium	105	**Db** - Dubnium
16	**S** - Sulfur	46	**Pd** - Palladium	76	**Os** - Osmium	106	**Sg** - Seaborgium
17	**Cl** - Chlorine	47	**Ag** - Silver	77	**Ir** - Iridium	107	**Bh** - Bohrium
18	**Ar** - Argon	48	**Cd** - Cadmium	78	**Pt** - Platinum	108	**Hs** - Hassium
19	**K** - Potassium	49	**In** - Indium	79	**Au** - Gold	109	**Mt** - Meitnerium
20	**Ca** - Calcium	50	**Sn** - Tin	80	**Hg** - Mercury	110	**Ds** - Darmstadtium
21	**Sc** - Scandium	51	**Sb** - Antimony	81	**Tl** - Thallium	111	**Rg** - Roentgenium
22	**Ti** - Titanium	52	**Te** - Tellurium	82	**Pb** - Lead	112	**Cn** - Copernicium
23	**V** - Vanadium	53	**I** - Iodine	83	**Bi** - Bismuth	113	**Nh** - Nihonium
24	**Cr** - Chromium	54	**Xe** - Xenon	84	**Po** - Polonium	114	**Fl** - Flerovium
25	**Mn** - Manganese	55	**Cs** - Cesium	85	**At** - Astatine	115	**Mc** - Moscovium
26	**Fe** - Iron	56	**Ba** - Barium	86	**Rn** - Radon	116	**Lv** - Livermorium
27	**Co** - Cobalt	57	**La** - Lanthanum	87	**Fr** - Francium	117	**Ts** - Tennessine
28	**Ni** - Nickel	58	**Ce** - Cerium	88	**Ra** - Radium	118	**Og** - Oganesson
29	**Cu** - Copper	59	**Pr** - Praseodymium	89	**Ac** - Actinium		
30	**Zn** - Zinc	60	**Nd** - Neodymium	90	**Th** - Thorium		

List of the 118 elements in the periodic table by atomic number.